Tormentil and Bleached Bones

must we always go
on a voyage or adventure
at last to discover
the vein of darkness running through
the routine and the known

Tormentil and Bleached Bones

Thomas A. Clark

Polygon

EDINBURGH

ACKNOWLEDGEMENTS

Thanks are due to Moschatel Press, Morning Star Publications, Prest Roots Press and Verse, where some of these poems first appeared.

© Thomas A. Clark 1993

Published by Polygon
22 George Square
Edinburgh

Set in Linotron Sabon
by Koinonia, Bury and
printed and bound in
Great Britain by
Short Run Press, Exeter

British Library Cataloguing in
    Publication Data
Clark, Thomas A.
    Tormentil and Bleached Bones
    I. Title
    821. 914

ISBN 0 7486 6168 9

The Publisher acknowledges
subsidy from the Scottish Arts
Council towards the publication
of this volume.

THROUGH WHITE VILLAGES

Andalucia, Winter 1988

a land of surfaces bearing light
bright sunlight, dust on the road
a dead sheep among periwinkles
a village like snow on the sierra
forts and frontiers, heights and sanctuaries
in every village a different air
the eyes open, the heart unguarded
morning, noon and evening

the olive grove in the white village
white egrets on the rocks
a fire of gorse and rosemary
the deep song in the narrow street
a street that climbs the mountainside
the virgin of remedies
air with the clarity of a bell
the stunning purity of the walls

the feminine light of the masculine sun
nothing moving but a buzzard
broken glass and wild irises
the bread warm, the wine sweet
crags like brigands lurking in cloud
slowly making a shape on the map
the monastery bell and the goat bell
talking in an orchard as the light fades

walking south from grey to green
beating the olive branches
old sorrow, new pain
coffee and cognac
plunging my head beneath a waterfall
the lift of a small breeze
the gloom beneath the cork trees
a donkey tethered in the dusk

in every village a different light
water lapping at marble
burial chambers in the castle walls
austerity and passion
a long afternoon without shadow
the bitterness of distance
a goatherd among goats and rocks
rough tracks to other villages

a haze of almond blossom
eating breakfast and looking at Africa
above the valley, beneath the vines
a gift of oranges
a road fringed with greetings
walking among colours
leaving every thought behind
the sea slowly filling the horizon

THE HOMECOMING

the true south and the upland grass
the bright glade and the fallen lintel
the driving rain and the sudden calm
the fiddle tune and the rowan berries
the ruined chapel and the black water

the hard road and the steady light
the heat haze and the peat smoke
the pebble bed and the yellow flag
the grey song and the fault line
the dog rose and the meeting place

the keen air and the pine needles
the furze blossom and the brown trout
the far hills and the broken boat
the bleached bones and the summer dwelling
the slack tide and the raised beach

the blue sky and the summit cairn
the hanged crow and the sheep dip
the bracken fronds and the healing pool
the lobster pots and the teasel patch
the old fort and the malt whisky

the scree slope and the circling buzzard
the lonely glen and the heather fire
the sphagnum moss and the golden lichen
the bladder wrack and the shell mound
the west wind and the last harebell

the lark notes and the ripe brambles
the tweed jacket and the grouse moor
the barbed wire and the holy island
the standing stone and the loud burn
the wild goats and the bog myrtle

PATHS AND FRUITS

to set out early
　　with no destination
with the gorse in flower
　　with perhaps a light rain

to take the short path
　　towards delight or harm
the beards of the ripe barley
　　caressing your bare arm

to wander, linger
  digress and forget
to be full in response
  to be able to wait

to waste time watching
  raindrops in a pool
make small circles lasting
  no time at all

to approximate less
    to oak and rock
than to air, mist
    water, smoke

to talk and to listen
    and to turn on your heel
to steady yourself
    on the curve of the hill

to work again at your own
    half-articulated tune
to be as glad in the rain
    as a mountain burn

to sleep in the sunshine
    a sleep as light as air
to be alone and lonely
    for a mile or more

to go on and on
    expecting nothing
to be everywhere transparent
    displacing nothing

to feel while the wind
    howls over stones
or tears at the meadow grasses
    quiet in your bones

to pause before entering
 a stand of trees
to splash your face with water
 and then lift it to the breeze

to slowly unravel
 the knots of desire
that bind up distances
 of cold and fire

to take the stile
   beside the open gate
that leads to a profusion
   of flowers and light

to leap across the waters
   of a swift-flowing stream
to sit beside it, to step
   in and out of time

to clear a small space
    between stimulus and response
to stare into the haze
and watch an oak tree dance

to detach yourself from
    each form and event
until the days take on
    depth, clarity, extent

FROM SEA TO SEA

Across Southern Italy
from the Mediterranean to the Adriatic
Winter 1989

brilliance, rustling in frost
only one traveller on the road
light pouring through every gap
every surface unstable
from the sea to the mountains
the madonna of the snows
boulders strewn across the path
village lights among the stars

shivering in the early light
a young foal blinking and shivering
gunfire echoing, quiet settling
all morning small avalanches
kicking a stone for half a mile
a favourite tune in a foreign land
soldiers loitering on the edge of a wood
hard snow sweetening the air

lizards and bees among crocuses
seven dirty sheep in a bumpy blue van
a new town on the site of an earthquake
the song of the fish-seller
prayers recited in the market place
the simple kindness of good wishes
having a destination but no plans
my footsteps among the ruins

high bare fields with larks above them
a valley hung with hazel catkins
roads like rivers, roads like scars
cool beer at the crossroads
the variable estimates of distance
the warm light in the cave dwellings
a clear head and a ragged shadow
dark breathing earth

a seamless sky over slow hills
farms abandoned among cypresses
the birthplace of a classical poet
a meal in a dark room
the walls spread like flowers for the light
widows strolling on the outskirts of town
leaving all the litter behind
dead robin, dead blue tit, dead warbler

long miles of heat and dust
a bonfire of olive trimmings
remembering and forgetting
joining the flow of the crowd
washing hung from palace windows
afternoon, the debris of the carnival
nets being mended in the sun
the sea, the sky, the cathedral

COIRE FHIONN LOCHAN

lapping of the little waves
breaking of the little waves
spreading of the little waves
idling of the little waves

rippling of the little waves
settling of the little waves
meeting of the little waves
swelling of the little waves

trembling of the little waves
dancing of the little waves
pausing of the little waves
slanting of the little waves

tossing of the little waves
scribbling of the little waves
lilting of the little waves
sparkling of the little waves

leaping of the little waves
drifting of the little waves
running of the little waves
splashing of the little waves

BEINN FUAR

where the path gives out
among glacial debris
droppings of mountain hares
above the cliffs above the sea
a great skua scolds from a rock
the hours drop away
winds blow up from nowhere
I forget my own shape

rowan scrub huddles
out of the biting wind
salix thrives in ravines
exposed ledges erode
I follow the wind furrows
it is cold the sky is clear
large contours spread before me
glitter of rock and water

high up the moor
is ringed with crags
dark presences that brood
or retire behind cloud
it is good to walk
for hours in the silence
good to sit for a while inside
the din of falling water

all day in shadow
in silence and cold
tumbled rocks piled up
a dance among disasters
at the head of the glen
ice crystals in grit
I climb onto the edge
to leagues of light and air

today all the tints
of grey are nourished
by a gentle rain
each thing is extended
in tenderness beyond
its own outline
hill moistened into sky
birch into larch wood

on the edge of the forest
a moment of hesitation
the trees crowd together
the stillness is complete
am I bold enough to enter
the moment stretches out
deep moss beneath pines
a few shards of cold light

ruins of summer dwellings
crofts overrun with bracken
remains of chimney breasts
gables to the wind
sheep grazing in doorways
daffodils fallen lintels
a few broken bottles
I shelter by a wall

stooping to drink
in a parenthesis of rock
thyme-scented water
from an iron cup
so cold so cold
it burns the throat
a draught of clarity
on an old hill road

the tide sifts through
shell fragments and skulls
on cliffs above the sea
sheep carcasses rot
rain-washed sun-bleached
strewn across the tundra
are bones more delicate
than ling or tormentil

cloud covers the cairn
everything closes in
chill numbs the fingers
on the mountain's shoulder
wind increases to a gale
walk forward lie flat
wait to steady a beating heart
run down to sunlight

in the ponderous heat
of noon might run
a thrill of breeze
through tall bracken
a lack of concern
as cool as the belly
of a small frog sitting
in the palm of my hand

walking a raised beach
picking among stones
strolling along leaping
away from the tide
stretched out in marram grass
staring up into blue
no footprints but my own
going down to the sea

in the early afternoon
the path comes down to a lake
I stop for a while and watch
the movement of the little waves
waves spreading and subsiding
running with the lightest breeze
sound lapping at the silence
the moment rippling out

strolling down a great glen
tired slightly drunk
the roar of water rises
silence closes in behind
hills flatten to a plane
a long day of rough terrain
deep in muscle and bone
an ache like stored light

in the thickening gloom
hold a grass blade
between your thumbs
and filling your cheeks
blow across its edge
like an animal in pain
the sound will bring
every shadow to attention

stretched out above the bay
where do I end and where begin
at the disposal of a gravity
that bears me up and pins me down
cliffs collapse into the sea
hours yawn blood circulates
my head lolls back in the heather
my figure is dispersed in sky

meeting another
on a lonely road
a nod a greeting
perhaps a few words
the gorse in flower
we accompany each other
for a mile or more
after we have parted

on the beach after storm
most delicate seaweeds
feathers of water ripples
rock pools full of calm
a wounded guillemot
pulling itself over
the litter of boulders
a new front coming in

early a trickle of stones
released by light from ice
the bellowing of a stag
cold air in the nostrils
at each step a recovery
of range and resilience
looking out over islands
rum from a hip flask

at a turn in the glen
I am suddenly away
from the sound of waves
I am suddenly alone
in the stillness wondering
what else there might be
so constant and familiar
I no longer notice it

the little one of the stones
the clachoran the wheatear
restless flitting bobbing
I watch it in the heather
caught between impulses
lighting lifting hovering
its note is like two stones
struck lightly together

what carries over
from every movement
slips ahead to watch
the movement fade
the grace that glides
free from each shape
is the proper guardian
of every step

light is thrown back by water
the rocks are hard and clear
but appear insubstantial
surfaces contrived for light
with the greatest composure
I could reach out and put
my clear but insubstantial
hand right through them

a large boulder resting
against a young juniper
water plunging off
a ledge into space
wild flowers clinging
to corrie and scree
itinerant passing through
gently I take the slope

ABOUT NOTHING IN PARTICULAR

to make a short song
out of nothing, a few words
to keep me going
to take nothing's notation
is a mile's occupation

the thistle and gorse
the kiss, the blessing, the curse
are built on nothing
the cairn, the old fort, the hill
the tibia of the gull

that water is best
that bubbles up out of rock
tasting of nothing
in a lull in a cold wind
I have stretched out to drink it

convolvulus stems
the complexities of thought
old country dances
weave figures around nothing
bring plenitude from nothing

you are my good friend
the best of company on
the long shore road home
when there is nothing to say
you stay quiet and easy

just before the dawn
I woke to the sound of rain
and knowing nothing
of my location or shape
like the grass I was refreshed

FOREST, MOUNTAIN, CITY

Portugal,
Winter 1990

the sacred way through the forest
arriving at the proper pace
mist closing every vista
the convent bell in the steady rain
thin webs trembling on lichen
cypress, bay, arbutus, tree fern
around and around the same problem
coming out onto the hillside

a woman balancing a water pitcher
mimosa blossom floating on a lake
white rhododendron petals floating
reflections of red rhododendron
a waterboatman plying between ripples
a pale green frog leaping in
folded lilies, unfolded lilies
water dripping from a satyr's lip

mountain line above cloud line
perfume of mimosa, brimstone butterfly
a pregnant woman looking over a valley
rough dark country wine
sweet crocuses in wild places
the balanced rock
shapes of hills, modes of feeling
blue gentians on red earth

the wind hones its edge on stone
walking, thinking, looking, walking
strip fields, stone grain stores
fresh young green in pools
pines slashed to collect resin
bright, bright, says a little bird
irrigation channels overflowing
grit, rubble, surfacing in dreams

looking over the roofs to the river
strong light producing tears
people together, people alone
smells of urine and fried fish
mistakes with language, surprises
a haircut, not too short
the evening stroll among lights and music
street dogs heading home

morning on buildings like cliff faces
straight avenues, winding streets
the great piles of dried cod
crochet on the tram ride
a man fitting dovetail jointing
placing change in an outstretched hand
peacocks under ancient olive trees
gulls above the police sirens

SOME DETAILS OF HEBRIDEAN
HOUSE CONSTRUCTION

the walls are built with
unmortared boulders
the external faces having
an inward slope
the corners rounded

roofs are thatched with
straw, ferns or heather
and weighted with stones
hung from heather ropes

instead of overhanging
the roof is set back
on a broad wall-top
which in the course of time
becomes mantled with
grass and verdure
which may provide
occasional browsing
for a sheep or goat

back to the wind
face to the sun
is the general
orientation

the floor is of beaten earth
and the main room is reached
by way of the byre
there are no windows and
the frugal flame of the peat
gives the only illumination
smoke wanders and finds
egress by a hole in the roof

in the outer isles the floor is covered
with white sand from the machair

a few steps ascend
the wall near the door
to enable the roof
to be thatched or roped
or the family to sit
in the summer weather
and sew, chat or knit

by the peat store
near to the doorway
is placed a large stone
for the wanderer to sit on

RIASG BUIDHE

*A visit to the island of Colonsay,
Inner Hebrides, April 1987*

There are other lives we might lead, places we might get to know, skills we might acquire.

When we have put distance between ourselves and our intentions, the sensibility comes awake.

Every day should contain a pleasure as simple as walking on the machair or singing to the seals.

The ripples on the beach and the veins in the rocks on the mountain show the same signature.

When we climb high enough we can find patches of snow untouched by the sun, parts of the spirit still intact.

The grand landscapes impress us with their weight and scale but it is the anonymous places, a hidden glen or a stretch of water without a name, that steal the heart.

The mere sight of a meadow cranesbill can open up a wound.

We live in an age so completely self-absorbed that the ability to simply look, to pour out the intelligence through the eyes, is an accomplishment.

You will require a tune for a country road, for hill walking a slow air.

When I climb down from the hill I carry strands of wool and fronds of bracken on my clothing, small barbs of quiet in my mind.

At dawn and again at dusk we feel most acutely the passing of time but at dawn the world is with us while at dusk we stand alone.

The farther we move from habitation, the larger are the stars.

There is a kind of bagpipe and fiddle music, practised in a gale, which is full of distance and longing.

A common disease of sheep, the result of cobalt deficiency, is known as 'pine'.

The best amusement in rain is to sit and watch the clouds negotiate the mountain.

Long silences are as proper in good company as a song on a lonely road.

Let everything you do have the clean edge of water lapping in a bay.

In any prevailing wind there are small pockets of quiet: in a rock pool choked with duckweed, in the lee of a cairn, in the rib-cage of a sheep's carcass.

When my stick strikes a stone, it is a call to order.

The most satisfying product of culture is bread.

In a landscape of Torridonian sandstone and heather moor, green and gold lichens on the naked rock will ignite small explosions of sensation.

Whatever there is in a landscape emerges if we just sit still.

It is not from novelty but from an unbroken tradition that real human warmth can be obtained, like a peat fire that has been rekindled continuously for hundreds of years.

After days of walking on the moor, shoulders, spine and calves become resilient as heather.

The hardest materials are those which display the most obvious signs of weathering.

We can carry a tent, food, clothing or the world on our shoulders, but how light we feel when we lay them down.

Just to look at a beach of grey pebbles can cool the forehead.

On a small island, the feeble purchase that the land obtains between the sea and the sky, the drifting of mist and the intensity of light, unsettles the intellect and opens the imagination to larger and more liquid configurations.

Although the days should extend in a graceful contour, the hours should not be accountable.

A book of poems in the rucksack – that is the relation of art to life.

On a fine day, up on the heights, with heat shimmering from the rocks, I can stretch out on my back and watch all the distances dance.

The duty of the traveller, wherever he finds himself, is always to keep faith with the air.

We should nurture our own loneliness like an Alpine blossom.

Solitude and affection go well together – to work alone the whole day and then in the evening sit round a table with friends.

To meet another person on a walk is like coming to a river.

In the art of the great music, the drone is eternity, the tune tradition, the performance the life of the individual.

It is on bare necessity that lyricism flourishes best, like a cushion of moss campion on granite.

When the people are gone, and the house is a ruin, for long afterwards there may flourish a garden of daffodils.

The routines we accept can strangle us but the rituals we choose give renewed life.

When the lark sings and the air is still, I sometimes feel I could reach over and take the island in my hand like a stone.

THE CASTLES OF THE GOOD

In the land of the Cathars
Languedoc, France, Winter 1991

morning, a man carrying flowers
a greeting, a handshake
light on wrought iron balconies
quiet courtyards, squalid streets
picking my way through the suburbs
the distances between sounds
eucalyptus and mimosa by a river
the mistral blowing in the darkness

scrub, thorn and herb
the exposed fabric of the earth
rents and fissures in rock and cloud
the cutting edge of the wind
a path through a juniper wood
boots weighted with mud
the castle on the pierced rock
breath held above a sheer drop

a path through a beech wood
broom, saxifrage, hellebore
rock perishing, tough growth persisting
old borders no longer held
the breached defenses of cloud
the chapel poised on the cliff edge
in low visibility, absolute clarity
a silence older than stone

skeins of cloud, threads of rain
the hermitage in the gorge
walking by the river, listening
a stillness older than water
the scent of stacked timber
hard snow under fir trees
standing under fir trees, listening
repeated notes, brittle little songs

peaks like slow white waves
a blue light over snow
biting the cold
directions from a shepherdess
sheep bells on winter pasture
an old wound suddenly open
the consolation of the air

white lifted up to blue
healing warmth and cleansing cold
the view from the battlements
the field where the faithful burned
lavender honey
flowers, butterflies, a slow thaw
the quiet of backstreets at noon
the fluttering of pigeons

BY KILBRANNAN SOUND

the glare of a black stone
the gleam of a black stone
the glimmer of a black stone
the glint of a black stone
the glitter of a black stone
the gloss of a black stone
the gloom of a black stone
the glow of a black stone

The rythmns and details of the landscape, the clarity that comes with walking and the stillness that comes from turning aside – these are the main ingredients in Tom Clark's poetry.

While the poems return to Clark's native Scotland and to the Hebrides, the present volume also includes winter walks in Italy, Andalucia and elsewhere.

Clark's poems have appeared in numerous publications in Britain, the US and continental Europe, and in small editions from his own Moschatel Press.

THOMAS A. CLARK was born in Greenock in 1944 and now lives in Nailsworth, Gloucestershire. With his wife, Laurie, he runs Cairn Gallery, a centre for contemporary art.

ISBN 0-7486-6168-9

9 780748 661688

£6.95

Polygon 22 George Square Edinburgh EH8 9LF